FINANCIAL LOGINS

Fidelity Investments (Roth IRA)

USER: Oftheeoaks
password: swr?Pa.W26KYcj

Ally Bank (High Yield Savings Account)